Wearing glasses

CONTENTS

Why do we need glasses?

Lots of people wear glasses.

Glasses help them see things clearly.

Short sight

Some people are short sighted.
They can see nearby things well,
but distant things look blurred.

Short sighted people wear glasses to see distant things clearly.

Long sight

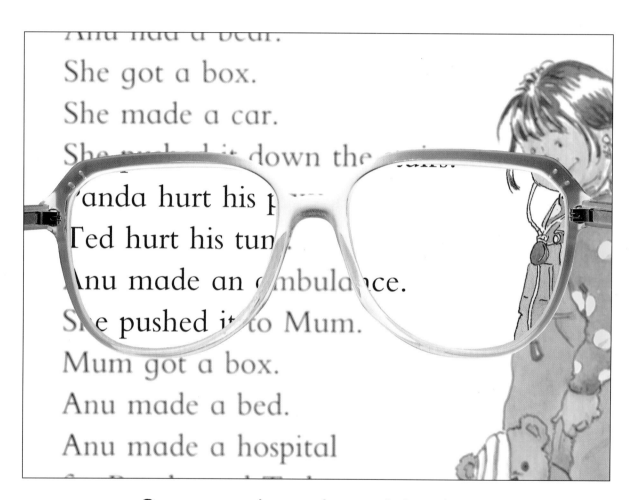

She got a box.
She made a car.
She ... it down the ...
...anda hurt his ...
Ted hurt his tun...
Anu made an ambulance.
She pushed it to Mum.
Mum got a box.
Anu made a bed.
Anu made a hospital

Some people are long sighted.
They can see distant things well,
but nearby things look blurred.

Long sighted people wear glasses to see nearby things clearly.

Lenses

lenses

frame

Glasses have two lenses and a frame.
The frame holds the lenses in front of the eyes.

The lenses are made from glass or clear plastic.
A powerful lens is more curved than a weak lens.

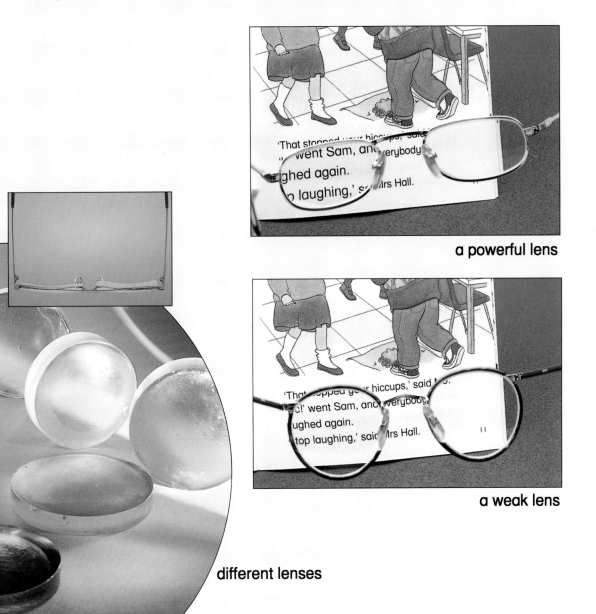

a powerful lens

a weak lens

different lenses

Visiting the optician

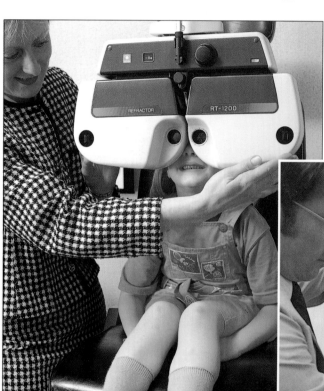

An optician tests people's eyes to see if they need glasses.

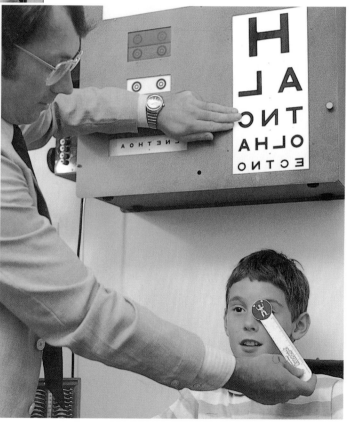

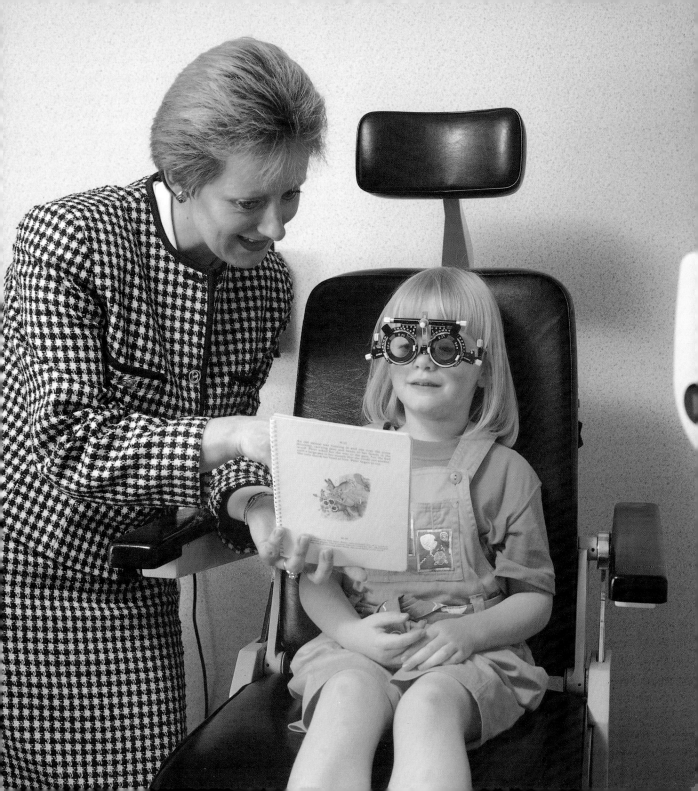

Choosing frames

There are lots of different frames.
You can choose a pair that suits you.

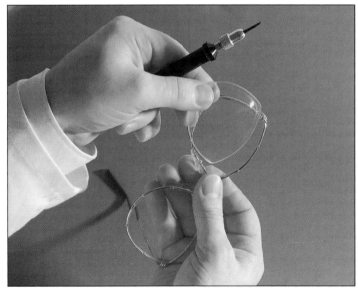

A technician cuts the lenses and fits them into the frames.

Eye protection

Eyes are easily damaged.
Glasses can keep people's eyes safe as well
as helping them to see.

sunglasses